MAKE EVERY THOUGHT PAY YOU A PROFIT

A BILLIONAIRE'S MINDSET

MAKE EVERY THOUGHT PAY YOU A PROFIT

By
JOHN ALAN ANDREWS

Copyright © 2024 by John A. Andrews
ISBN **9798879686562**
Cover Art:: ALI
Cover Photo: Adrian Carr All rights reserved.

All rights reserved.

Make every thought, every fact, that comes into your mind make you a profit. Make it work and produce for you. Think of things not as they are but as they might be. Don't merely dream - but create!

Robert Collier

INTRODUCTION

If we think about wealth we're apt to reap abundance. "As a man thinketh in his heart so is he." According to James Allen, the great philosopher. Applicably, if we think of poverty we'll reap lack.

We were not all born to make thoughts of profit lead us to the pot of gold. Even though, we have an inclination that the pot of gold exists. Most of us weren't fortunate enough to have wealth passed on to us. Even so, we all have the power to attract wealth. So, why aren't we striving to acquire such? Are we inundated with the thought: The rich get richer, and the poor get poorer? While the thought of lifting ourselves by our bootstraps lays wastefully inside our mindsets.

Yet, the truism echoes: we can change our destiny and, yes, you can become the person you desire to become by changing your thoughts. Is it going to be easy? Probably not, effective change never evolves like the Jack Beanstalk scenario.

It's more like a seasonal transition. During autumn, leaves die and fall to the ground before winter steps in, and like the seasons, change is a process. Real change doesn't happen overnight. It takes personal commitment.

Changing your thoughts and turning them into profit will take work, as does raising a child, building a successful marriage, getting a degree, or mastering a craft. Is it possible? It has been done. Ask any self-made Billionaire. According to Scot Anderson in his book Think Like A Billionaire - Become A Billionaire: *You want to be around people who pull you up. Not drag you down. People who push you to do more, not those who are jealous when you get more. You want to get around people who want to change themselves, not just change spouses and channels. You want to get around people who want to change the neighborhood, the city, the nation, the world. You don't want big talkers; you want to get around big doers. If I become who I am around, then I need to get around people who are headed towards success., not headed towards retirement.* And Ben Franklin said, "Associate with people who enjoy the measure of prosperity you would like to enjoy."

About your associations, Philosopher and Autor – W. Clement Stone said, *Be careful the environment you choose, for it will shape you, be careful the friends you choose, for you will become like them.*

There's truth to this maxim: "Show me your friends and I'll tell you who you are." If you spend time together with bank robbers you could end up driving the getaway car, and if you associate with pigs, you'll soon be rolling in the mud. Kids who wind up in gangs join them primarily to fulfill a need for community, and soon, they prey on society to support that community and attain identity within the group. Through conversion to Christianity, though, a gangbanger can dust himself off to lead a church or become a mentor to struggling youth.

Paul, once a persecutor of Christians, encountered a changed life on the road to Damascus when struck by a bright light from heaven. Following three days of blindness, he regained his sight by the hand of a disciple named Ananias, and immediately turned his life around, preaching Jesus as the Son of God (Acts 9:1-20).

Can you do it? Only if you think you can. Will you lift yourself by your bootstraps? Leaders aren't born; they are made. Is the change worth the effort? Real change starts on the inside. According to James Allen, "You cannot travel within and stand still without." Your greatest achievement was at first, and for some time, just a thought.

One thing is for sure: If you grasp and apply this concept, that I'm about to give you, not only will you climb to insurmountable heights in your life and career, but you'll also have more joy, more friends, more love, more money, more passion, and a deep sense of spiritual and intellectual satisfaction. Fish will overflow your ship and others like in the parable when Jesus admonished his disciples to cast their nets on the other side.

As your guide, I must prepare you with simple guidelines. After receiving the idea to draft this book, inspirational thoughts flooded my mind, allowing me to urgently draft this chronicle – a follow-up to *Atomic Steps*.

To get the most out of it, you need passion, blended with a burning desire to change your thoughts and have them pay you an enormous profit.

Robert Collier admonishes, *Make every thought, every fact, that comes into your mind make you a profit. Make it work and produce for you. Think of things not as they are but as they might be. Don't merely dream - but create!*

Make this book your reading companion for the next 21 days. It is believed that one can make or break a habit in 21 days. Most people are content with doing just average. Become bullish and push yourself to read it daily for the next 30 days and write your new thoughts that you want to turn into PROFIT in the charts provided at the end of this book.

BILLIONAIRES DO WHAT MOST PEOPLE ARE N'T WILLING TO DO DAILY.
SEE YOU AT THE TOP!

*The oak sleeps in the acorn; the bird waits in its
egg; and in the highest vision of the soul
a waking angel stirs.*

— James Allen

1
CHANGE YOUR THOUGHTS

Philosopher, James Allen states, "Man is made or unmade by himself; in the armory of thought he forges the weapons by which he destroys himself; he also fashions the tools by which he builds for himself heavenly mansions of joy and strength and peace."
What is thought? Thought is a mental action that influences the world around us. Much like we see electricity at work, we see manifestations of thought

everywhere. It functions as a sort of wireless electricity. Thought is revealed in the actions of children, adults, and animals. It acts as a terrific force with unlimited power.

The electricity found therein can at times transfer that thought across countries as well as continents. If you are reading this book in a room or anywhere outdoors within a stone's throw from civilization, take a look around. You'll realize that you're looking at objects — including the book in your hands — created from someone's thoughts. All that you see on the outside first comes from within. Thought is the one thing over which you have absolute control; only you can decide what you do with your thoughts. Thus, influencing your way of thinking.

Your way of thinking starts with individual thoughts, whether good, bad, or ugly. Your subconscious produces thought, and your five senses give birth to thought based on your present environment. Whether you cultivate Godly or Satanic thoughts – you are at the helm. Anyway, be careful what you cultivate. The latter could like homing pigeons come back to haunt you. God and the devil are the two other sources of thought.

The five senses deal with the mind, but God deals with the heart and speaks to us through the Holy Spirit. After Jesus' ascension into heaven, his disciples received the outpouring of the Holy Spirit from God and thus performed miraculous deeds. "God says: 'In the last days I will pour out of my Spirit on all kinds of people. Your sons and daughters will prophesy. Your young men will see visions, and your old men will dream dreams.'" (Acts 2:17) In most cases, the mind has to be ready to utilize thoughts from God, just like the ground has to be prepared before seeds are sown therein.

Thoughts enter your mind whether you want them to or not. They arrive at every waking and sleeping moment of your life, as both initial data and original ideas and sometimes turn into action. In his book *Hung by the Tongue*, author Francis P. Martin explains, "An imagination is intent to do something about what you've been thinking; a stronghold is when the choice is not yours anymore, but you have submitted your will to the thought." Imaginations are images, and strongholds are responsible for turning thoughts into reality. Once a thought arrives, the imagination works on it, and if a monopoly is placed on it, that thought becomes reality.

Let's say, for instance, that the thought of stealing comes to mind. It's up to you to dismiss or keep that thought. If you choose to entertain the thought, it will become an imagination, or intent to steal. If that thought is caressed, it will evolve into a stronghold and you will end up stealing, unless you submit the temptation to the power of God and, with His help, avoid yielding to it.

It would be best if you decided what you're going to do with a thought. Will you discard it, throwing it into your recycle bin, or will you employ it? The thoughts you utilize will shape your destiny — either a life of mediocrity or a life of greatness. Evidence of the latter is seen in the lives of Columbus, Copernicus, Gandhi, Winston Churchill, Mother Teresa, Abraham Lincoln,

Martin Luther King Jr., Helen Keller, and many others, who, out of their thoughts, accomplished great things. Imagine what would have happened to our civilization if they had discarded those thoughts. In his book *How to Be A Genius Billionaire* Michael Christopher Lloyd states: *What the mind can see, a man can do.*

2

DISCARDED THOUGHTS

It is a given that our world is full of hidden information. However, more often than not, thoughts traverse various minds. Unfortunately, and fortunately, thoughts that aren't utilized could be counted as discarded by the recipient of the thought.

Both poverty and riches are the offspring of thought, author Napoleon Hill says in his book *Think and Grow Rich.*

If you're not careful, abandoned thoughts can come back to haunt you. Have you ever given up a thought or idea that came to you, only to later see it achieved by someone else? Because a thought came to you, it technically doesn't mean that you own such unless you put it in play.

People frequently tell me they have a great idea for a screenplay. My usual response is, "Why don't you write it or have someone else assist in drafting it for you?" But nine times out of 10, they fall asleep on the idea, allowing it to elude their grasp, only to later watch it unfold on the movie screen. They then pound their fists - *darn it was my idea!*

On the other hand, you're constantly bombarded by negative thoughts that, if entertained, will hurt the way you do life. Those thoughts — ones that belittle, dehumanize, and keep you in bondage — are the ones you must change. It would be best if you let go of thoughts that tell you that you came from nothing, will never amount to anything, and are no good. "What makes you think you have it in you to accomplish anything worthwhile?" those thoughts say. "You failed yesterday, and you are destined to fail again today." "You don't have what it takes to make it happen." And on and on…

The truth is nobody has ever accomplished anything worthwhile without changing those kinds of condescending thoughts.

When I was a little boy growing up on the islands of Saint Vincent and the Grenadines, my mom would say, very philosophically: *What you give out in your right hand you're going to receive in your left. You can do whatever you set in your heart and mind to accomplish. If you can think it, you can do it.*

For a while, I thought she was too immersed in the Word. But some of it did resonate in my delicate mind.

When you have something good you don't play with it. You don't take chances with it. You don't take risks with it. When you have something good, you give it everything you can. Because when you take care of something good. That something good takes care of you.

- Anonymous

3

TURNING THOUGHTS INTO REALITY

I was obsessed with becoming a police officer when I grew up, for example, so I studied policemen and prayed to God that someday I would become one. Today, the profession doesn't intrigue me in the same way it used to, but most of the screenplays and novels I've authored are about police officers or have something to do with law enforcement or police procedural. What my mother told me as a child, I've realized, has merit. Thoughts hold magic and power and can be realized.

As a dad, I make it a habit to tell my three sons, now ages 28, 26, and 23, not only that I love them and am proud of them, but also that they can do anything they can imagine. They believe in their ability and, as a result, the two eldest have already embarked upon the task of collaboratively writing their first Disney-type screenplay. They are developing the will to win as creatives.

During the Cannes Film Festival of 2023, I visited Nice and Monaco, nearby regions of Southern France. On this trip, I caught the vision for drafting a twisted Crime thriller, cemented in the enclaves of those three cities.

Before the Cannes Festival wrapped, I found myself sitting in a room where studio execs were poised to discuss Filming in those localities and on the studio lot. I asked myself: *Was this happening?*

It was my fourth meeting of the day, and after the third meeting, I said to myself:

I've had enough lecturing for one day. It is time to return to my booth and entertain prospective clients. After all, that's why I attended the event, I reckoned.

Even so, I felt belonged and sat in for meeting number four. You see, I have the voraciousness for the movie studio. You say movie studios and I am tickled – Quora.

The studio execs did their spiel. In my mind, the dots were connecting. I saw endless possibilities. My hand immediately went up when the speaker took a breather for questions. I proceeded by asking tough questions regarding the sustainability or longevity of that market and its packaging. If they were ready to launch out, so was I.

I returned to New York, and amid fighting off the naysayers of my vision, I went to work –drafting the police procedural thriller. As a result, in less than four months, I returned to France at the Studios' invitation and sat in for a meeting, a tour, plus a luncheon to discuss the upcoming TV series. It is said,

"Luck is where preparedness meets with opportunity."

When a champion wants something, they go after it with all they can muster. "Bring it on," he says. "Lead me through the unknown. There I will discover myself and others. If it has never been done, I will create it. If it demands training, I will become coachable. The tougher it becomes the better I like it. If it must be it is up to me. Therefore, I will "Man up." If I go down, it will not happen because I wimped out - If I go down, I'm going down fighting. I possess a "pit bull" mentality because I was born to win!" Champions look for something to latch on to, a dream, a vision, a cause.

"Give it to me and watch what I will do with it," they demand. If the team desires a touchdown, they crave the interception and cradle that ball into the end zone.

Ironically, that play may not have been drawn up or happenstance. However, it has been drafted and executed over and over again, analogous to the baby steps syndrome. Those steps eventually mature into "the catch me if you can" scenario

4

BELIEVE IT, CONCEIVE IT

In *Think and Grow Rich*, Hill talks about a secret hidden in the pages. If you're ready to receive it, he says, you already possess one half; you'll acquire the other half once it reaches your mind. This secret, he adds, cannot be had at any price by those who are not intentionally searching for it. So, I read the book in hot pursuit and with an open mind, believing to conceive. Ideas came to me in abundance, and I juggled them. My favorites? "Your thoughts and desires serve as the magnet which attracts units of life, from the great ocean of life out there." And "All achievement, all earned riches, have their beginning in an idea."

Belief is a powerful force that drives thought. Good thoughts are usually born out of inspiration, and to be inspired, you must be in alignment with God. At one point during Jesus' ministry, His disciples failed to cast a demon out of a little boy; they lacked faith. But Jesus rebuked the demon and he departed from the child. "Later, the disciples came to Jesus asking, 'Why couldn't we cast him out?' And Jesus said unto them, 'Because of your unbelief: for verily I say unto you, "If you have faith as a mustard seed, you shall say unto this mountain, 'Remove hence to yonder place;' and it shall remove;" and nothing shall be impossible unto you." (Matt. 17:19-20)

In the story of David and Goliath, David's peers probably saw a mountain standing in his way but his faith in the Lord produced an unexpected outcome in battle. "When Goliath looked at David and saw that he was only a boy, tanned and handsome, he looked down on David with disgust. He said, 'Do you think I am a dog, that you come at me with a stick?' He used his gods' names to curse David; He said to David, 'Come here I'll feed your body to the birds of the air and the wild animals!'

David said unto him, 'You come to me using a sword and

two spears. But I come to you in the name of the Lord All-Powerful, the God of the armies of Israel! You have spoken against him.'" (1 Sam. 17:42-45) David saw the giant as too big to miss and slew him with a few stones and a slingshot. David thought he could defeat Goliath and did just so.

Belief inspires one to do the seemingly impossible. An inspired person is apt to break bonds of restraint in his or her mind to accomplish tasks in a record-breaking style.

Through inspiration, Chicago Bulls player Michael Jordan pursued respect for himself and his team by scoring three times his jersey number as he dropped 69 points on the Cleveland Cavaliers in March 1990. Whenever you have an inspired thought, you must trust it and act on it.

5

THE WILL TO SUCCEED

After the Screen Actors Guild commercial strike in 1998, compounded by the effects of 9/11, I struggled as a commercial actor. Previously I'd had a very successful streak of national television spots, landing nine within 13 months. So off I went searching for ways to make things happen. I wasn't going to allow the industry drought to stop me.

Out of the universe, a hunch nudged me: "Why not become a filmmaker? That's what most successful people in Hollywood do." Some of my acquaintances were already climbing that ladder of success, so I submitted to the idea.

At the time, I had no experience in filmmaking, except that which I had picked up on a few movie sets. Nonetheless, I was determined to succeed. There was a classic 1970s film I liked so much that I thought about remaking it. For the next three weeks, I made phone calls to find out who held the rights to my intended pet project. When I finally contacted the studio, a woman answered the phone and told me they were not interested in selling the rights to a third party.

That statement didn't sit well with me. You see, my plane had already taken off, the fasten-your-seat-belt signs were already extinguished, and the hostess was serving the beverage of the day. I composed myself, contacted a writer friend whose script was recently optioned by a major studio, and asked him to assist me in writing my script. He did one of the best things a person can do for another: instead of giving me a fish, he showed me how to fish by sending me guidelines for writing a screenplay. I got busy. My mantra echoed, "I'll write my own. I'll show them. They'll be begging for my work someday." My imaginary airplane was swiftly gaining altitude.

The initial draft of that first screenplay was completed within 29 days. Later, I gladly showed one of my scripts to an acquaintance of mine who is a director. He not only told me I was such a novice but also said it was the worst screenplay he had ever seen. That hit home like a ton of bricks, and after a few sleepless nights, I went back to the drawing board. About a year later, he read one of my action thrillers and remarked,

"I think you have the knack, guy. Not too many people can do it this way."

Two of my original screenplays are currently in the pre-production phase, but that wouldn't have happened if I hadn't followed through with my thoughts and kept going. To date, I've written over 76 books, multiple screenplays as well as TV series. If I hadn't coupled belief with thought, my ideas might have been left in the recycle bin.

6

THOUGHTS LEFT IN THE RECYCLE BIN

John F. Kennedy, the youngest and one of the greatest United States presidents, said this: "The problems of the world cannot possibly be solved by the skeptics or cynics whose horizons are limited by the obvious realities. We need men who can dream of things that never were."

It should alarm you that the ideas that could beckon a revolution and solve most of the world's problems, including AIDS, cancer, and Alzheimer's disease, may be sitting idle in the recycle bins of people's minds. People who allow their thoughts to sit idle are content with inside-the-box thinking, filled with what I call "the could-have-been syndrome." That's the way millions of people live their lives. They create a worldwide "I don't have what it takes" epidemic; as one of my associates says, they have no guts.

Every business, building, highway, school, house, song, screenplay, relationship — everything — begins with a thought. In the book *The Magic of Thinking Big*, David Schwartz writes, "Think: 'I can do better.' The best is not unattainable. There's room for doing everything better. Nothing in the world is being done as well as it could be. And when you think, 'I can do better,' ways to do better will appear."[6] Thinking that way will ignite your creative powers and, like the pent-up flow released from a dam, you will become relentless.

7

USED THOUGHTS

In his book *The Magic of Believing*, Claude Bristol states, "There never was a period in history when we should study our thoughts more, try to understand them, and learn how to improve our position in life by drawing upon the great source of power that lies within each of us."

How can you tell which thoughts are good and which thoughts are bad? Think of the mind — your storehouse of thoughts — as an empty hard drive in a computer. It knows nothing except what you put into it. The real you are your heart, or your spirit, from where all issues of life flow. I've made it a habit for over a decade to feed my computer - the mind with "good" by reading and listening to inspirational material just before bed. Sometimes I fall asleep while listening. But because my subconscious is still awake while I sleep, it absorbs most of the information. I've noticed that at times throughout the day, inspirational thoughts and messages hit me. And more often than not, when I'm in a situation where it's crucial to find the right words, I'm able to deliver.

Upon acting on the idea to draft this book, I felt as if the floodgates of my heart and mind opened, pouring out a storehouse of inspiration. I was directed to previously read books in my library and even to the page, and the highlighted quote, needed for the appropriate insert.

When it comes to thought, only you can determine what is installed on your computer. Remember, input equals output. What you sow you shall also reap.

8

THINK OUTSIDE OF THE BOX

Thought largely determines the "haves" from the "have nots" in today's society. Author Victor Hugo said, "Nothing else in the world ... not all the armies ... is so powerful as an idea whose time has come."[8] And Warren Bennis, in his book *On Becoming a Leader*, writes, "A leader is, by definition, an innovator. He does things other people haven't done or don't do.

He does things in advance of other people. He makes new things. He makes old things new."

I believe we all can change what we touch for the better, and if we take advantage of our God-given potential, we'll leave this world a better place than we found it. After all, we were formed by the One who created everything; without Him, nothing was made. He loves always and gives bountifully when we serve Him in spirit and truth. If in His image we were formed and molded, why should we profess any form of inhibition? Why do we let small thinking control us? Could it be that we refrain from being plugged into the source — our infinite God? What happens to a river that refuses to draw water from its source?

If we think with a mindset of giving, we entertain abundance, and if we think with an attitude of withholding, we invite lack. The Bible states in Luke 6:38, "Give, and you will receive. You will be given much. Pressed down, shaken together, and running over, it will spill into your lap. The way you give to others is the way God will give to you." As the source gives to the stream so ought the stream to impart to the ocean.

In 1980, I was greeted by the Statue of Liberty, subway stations, taxis, and massive pedestrian traffic upon my entrance into New York City. A few years before, still living in the Islands, I had seen pictures of the city's greatest landmarks through a viewfinder on loan from a friend. I dreamed of living in the Big Apple, and I finally made it. After years of balancing odd jobs, seeds for my acting career were planted and took root.

While I drove taxis there in New York, my yearning to become an actor gnawed at me. One evening I picked up a passenger in Queens on his way to Manhattan, and we struck up a conversation. He said he was an actor and thought I had a great presence and would look powerful on screen. I told him I had been thinking about the possibility of acting for quite some time. Before exiting the cab, he not only gave me the name of his acting school and a contact person but also left his number in case I needed further assistance with my enrollment at Lee Strasberg Institute. The rest is history.

Moving to Los Angeles has, in many ways, broadened my horizons, enhanced my thinking, and expanded my vision. My experiences gained from "The University of Hard Knocks" have given me the idea and the drive to write, and today, this book is a result of that seed-planting-fruit-bearing thought.

The masses are known to sit back awaiting opportunities to show up. While those thoughts and images swirl around in their minds and are not brought to the drawing board.

Those thought images of inventions, concepts, and strategies elude them. They remain stuck at first base. Like the sailor sitting at the dock waiting for his ship to come in when it has not been sent out.

9

THE POWER OF THOUGHT

Claude Bristol states: in The Magic of Believing, "The secret of success lies not without, but within, the thoughts of man."
The sources of our drinking water are always heavily guarded and protected from intrusion and contaminants. People protect their bodies from the weather and other elements. And yet, few take the time to protect their thought source — the mind.

Imagine your best friend comes over to visit one day, and in his hands are two heavy bags. You offer him a seat, and then sit on your recliner and adjust it to a comfortable position. "What's in the bags?" you ask. He immediately opens one of them and deposits its contents, full of grime and filth, onto your nice clean carpet. As your nostrils react to the stench, he opens the other bag. Do you encourage him to dump more contaminants into your habitat? Of course not.

So, consider this example in terms of your mind. How do you treat the situation if a friend dumps garbage into your thought source? Do you say, "Thank you very much for the pollutants; could you please deposit some more?" or do you put the brakes on his toxin distribution extravaganza?

Napoleon Hill states in his book *Think and Grow Rich*, "It has been said that man can create anything which he can imagine."[11] Pascal had this to say: "Man's greatness lies in his power of thought."[12] Thoughts are magnetic. They will attract people who support them and an environment in which they can grow, producing after their kind.

You, too, can attract what you want, and the strength of the thought vibration will determine the strength of its attraction. A mere wish lacks the tenacity necessary to get unleashed.

By changing your thoughts, you will change your expressions, and eventually, your world. Everything you accomplish or fail to accomplish in life will be a direct result of the thoughts you cherish in your mind and the words that come out of your mouth. Wherever you are right now, everything you've experienced has prepared you for this moment in time.

Our achievements of today are but the total of our thoughts of yesterday. You are today where the thoughts of yesterday have brought you and will be tomorrow where the thoughts of today take you.
— Pascal

God spoke the world into existence

10

PROFITING FROM YOUR THOUGHTS

How many times have the idea come to you for a great book and you abandon it? Failing to realize that our industry is inundated with Ghostwriters, who if you are not able to, can assist in drafting that chronicle.

How many times have you seen a great piece of real estate investment and thought you were not up to the task of acquiring such? Only to see someone else grab that property and later turn it into profit. In the game of Monopoly, the player who lands on Park Avenue and builds hotels and houses on it, more often than not wins the game.

How many times have thoughts or images of an invention danced in your head and you abandoned the concept? Only to later see another individual cash in on the idea?

As a writer and filmmaker, I am enamored whenever a novel or screenplay title gets planted into my concentration... It is off to the races. *Where is my pen and paper? What is the setting? Who are my lead characters? What is the estimated budget? ... etc.* I'm hooked!

One day, my son Jefferri and I were heading to Chick-fil-A to grab a bite. Jeff began writing at age 9, and his brother Jonathan at age 11. It was quiet in his car. So, I asked him to find some music. I hoped an imaginary playlist would complement the abandoned cotton fields of South Carolina. The DJ dropped a Campaign AD. One word in the jingle began tugging at me.

"Jeff, that title will make a great horror film.

I interjected.

"True."

Jeff concurred.

Hours later, I found myself drafting my first horror project. In less than two months that book was published and is now not only generating revenue but is included in my current film slate which is moving toward development.

Just think of what a productive revolution would occur if we all acted on our ideas. The axiom screams: The mind is a terrible thing to waste. Yet, we throw our thoughts into an abyss.

If you are reading this book in a room or anywhere outdoors within a stone's throw from civilization, look around. You'll realize that you're looking at objects — including the book in your hands — created from someone's thoughts. All that you see on the outside first comes from within. Thought is the one thing over which you have absolute control; only you can decide what you do with your thoughts.

While working on the first draft of this book, I traveled to New York on a book-signing campaign for my latest title *Atomic Steps: Win Big or Go Home*. Ambling through La Guardia Airport, I ran into J. J. a debonair businessman, while waiting for the shuttle to my Hotel. We began a rapport after learning we were catching the shuttle to that same location. J. J. opened up and I soon learned that he is entrepreneurial, and currently working on multiple inventions. Not one or two but several. With patterned IPs, he felt comfortable sharing some details with me upon learning that we had common interests.

One of his ventures is revolutionary and is currently being funded.

J. J. and I again ran into each other at breakfast the following morning. He glowed with the idea of a TV show in conjunction with one of his inventions. J. J. is busily turning his thoughts into profit and on the road to success.

Refuse to let small thinking chart your course in life. David Schwartz states in *The Magic of Thinking Big*, "Nothing — absolutely nothing — in this world gives you more satisfaction than knowing you're on the road to success and achievement. And nothing stands as a bigger challenge than making the most of yourself."

Danforth exhorts in *I Dare You*, "I dare you to achieve something that will make the world point to you with even more pride than the present is pointing to those who have gone before you."

Danforth further challenges: *Are you content to have posterity look at your life so far and say, 'That is all he was capable of?' Or are you one of the priceless few, one of those with a restless feeling that someday you are going to climb to your rightful place of leadership? That someday you are going to create something worthy of your best.*

As you change your thoughts, success becomes imminent once you flip them into profit.

A definite purpose, held on to in the face of every discouragement and failure, despite all obstacles and opposition, will win no matter what the odds.

ROBERT COLLIER

11

WINNING THOUGHTS

Losers let things happen, but winners make things happen. Winners are never satisfied with who they are, and therefore, they're constantly changing and enhancing their self-image. They have a vision of the person they want to become, and they develop a well-defined, emotional picture of themselves as if they have already achieved that goal. Advance-winning pumps through their veins.

- They breathe the championship.

- They feel drenched from the entire bucket of Gatorade poured over their head.

- They experience the thrill of Disneyland before playing the Super Bowl.

- They caress the Oscar.

- They hear the crowd's approval.

- They feel the gold medal around their neck.

- They see a church with one million members worshipping in spirit and truth.

- They stand tall in the winner's circle.

- They feel their new self-image in advance.

- They dress and rehearse receiving the Nobel Prize.

Winners let nothing stand in the way of victory. You can smell their tenacity like expensive cologne because they have a feeling of their worth. They think, "I can, I will, and I shall not be denied."

The power of your purpose depends wholly on the vigor and determination behind it.

To paraphrase Dr. Bremer: Your resolute will and firm determination to succeed will carry you upstream, no matter how strong the current or how tough the obstacles in your way. But if your will is fragile and your determination wavering, you will float downstream with the multitudes of others who, like a dead fish, have not enough zest or willpower to force their way upstream.

Your aim needs to be as bold as your courage, not as timid as your fear. German poet Johann Wolfgang von Goethe said this:" Whatever you can do, or dream you can do, begin it. Boldness has genius, power, and magic in it."[12] Author James Allen stated, "Columbus cherished a vision of another world, and he discovered it; Copernicus fostered a vision of a multiplicity of worlds and a wider universe, and he revealed it."[13] Martin Luther King Jr. dreamed of an America where black kids and white kids would hold hands and walk together and it has happened. Humanity, though sometimes anti-visionary, never forgets its dreamers.

The man who has triumphed over difficulty — who has a vision and achieves it — bears signs of victory on his face. He seems to glow with triumph in every movement. The winner's circle embraces him.

Your decisions influence how you will live the remainder of your life. Choice precedes action as day precedes night. Life moves swiftly, and you need to act before you're acted upon.

What actions are you willing to take to impact your life positively? How strong is your courage? Do you want what you touch to turn to gold? Is there a thought seed you've sown with words of faith that you're now ready to prune and watch bear fruit? Are you ready to take some action?

This chapter, by far, is the most important in this book, and it's going to take some effort on your part. It's going to take giving up a humdrum life of lethargy for one of bravery and fun.
Most people are content to sit back and wait for things to come to them. You may have all the talent in the world, but if you're hiding your light under a bushel, the world won't know it. You will only attract the world by going to it with your shining light. The world has to know that you exist.

12

TIMELY ON THOUGHTS

Timing is everything. The famous axiom states: The "T" in timing is better than the "T" in talent. As I mentioned previously if your mom and dad did swing inadvertently you would have ended up in "no man's land." If the sun misses an appointment with planet Earth, we could for a long time be in utter darkness. If the waves miss their timing the ocean will swallow us up.

Timing has much to do with synchronicity but more so with preparedness. Successful people not only are adept at preparation. They rely on their intuition to capitalize on ideas. Therefore, whenever a great opportunity presents itself. They are all over it. Benjamin Disraeli says, "The secret of success in life is for a man to be ready for his time when it comes,"[2] Abraham Lincoln one of the biggest failures in life said:

"Give me six hours to chop down a tree, and I will spend the first four sharpening the axe."

Let me rephrase in case you missed it, when one is prepared and the right opportunity presents itself, he seizes it and dominates. That's what others call luck. In my opinion, which is Success 101 – the way a high achiever performs.

High achievers love what they do and are at their best doing so. They allow their creativity to operate at the maximum. Conversely, many people allow their creativity to be caged up by doing things they detest doing - simply because it pays the bills. I have seen people with so much potential waste it away behind a cubicle. They would rather be leveraged than leverage others. Many of the successful people I know today welcome business opportunities only if they have leverage. They want to know that they can build something and get paid continually whether they can perform or not. J. Paul Getty certainly understood this concept no wonder. He was the first recorded billionaire.

Today in America "leverage" the word of the wealthy has tremendous sex appeal. With so many layoffs' people are beginning to realize that they need more than having a job. I believe that one of the blessings derived from this recession will be a major entrepreneurial revolution – producing more entrepreneurs than any other economic downturn in our nation's history. My prediction is that the people who make that switch by thinking outside of the cubicle will produce more wealth than many others who have gone before them.

I was recently introduced to Arri, a very ambitious man in his 30s. He made a huge fortune back in his college days in the pager business – way in the millions. At one point, he almost got kicked out of his dorm because of the constant flow of clients. He later sold that business to get into the cell phone business. Very few people owned a cell phone - somewhat of two percent did back then. He was smart enough to place himself in front of that trend. In that business, he made millions and sold it to get into the DSL business when the dial-up was proven to be far too slow for graphics and the much larger files. He has also dominated that industry. Arri thrives on picking the right opportunity at the right time – he positioned himself in front of the trend rather than behind it.

Most successful people aren't lucky; they just master the law of timing. My movie producer friend amassed his fortune through a string of events. After his divorce, he later moved into an apartment complex managed by my ex-wife and me. He made his first big movie, which generated over $35M. It wasn't long before he moved out and bought a house in an upscale neighborhood. When the idea for the horror film was presented to him by a struggling producer who was office-less and sometimes officiated from my friend's office couch.

My friend sold that property, put some money down on another, and used a portion to finance the film. The film has grossed over $100M in its first and subsequent installments. He used his mindsight instead of his eyesight when he purchased that piece of property. His initial investment has now brought him an excess of over $500,000,000, within the last five years. Some said that he was lucky. I don't believe in luck. Real success occurs when preparedness and opportunity meet.

In his bestseller Rich Dad Poor Dad Investor and businessman Robert Kiyosaki talks about being a professional investor. He claims that the number one key is to find an opportunity that someone else missed. He writes "You see with your mind what others missed with their eyes."[4] Kiyosaki explains: A friend bought this run-down old house. It was spooky to look at. Everyone wondered why he bought it. What that man saw that we did not was that the house came with four extra empty lots. He realized that by going to the title company. After buying the house, the man tore it down and sold the five parcels to a builder for three times what he paid for the entire property. As a result, he made $75,000 for two months of work.5 He further explains: Great opportunities are not seen with your eyes. They are seen with your mind. Most people never get wealthy simply because they are not trained financially to recognize opportunities right in front of them.

As you strive to realize your vision, expect to be criticized and or called lucky. James Allen writes *The thoughtless, the ignorant, and the indolent, seeing the apparent effects of things and not the things themselves, talk of luck, of fortune, and of chance. Seeing others grow rich, they say, 'How lucky they are!' Observing others become intellectual, they exclaim, 'How highly favored they are!' And noting the saintly character and wide influence of still others, they remark, 'How chance aids them at every turn!' They do not see the trials and failures and struggles that these people have voluntarily encountered to gain their experience; have no knowledge of the sacrifices they have made, of the undaunted efforts they have put forth, of the faith they have exercised, that they might overcome the apparently insurmountable and realize the vision of their heart. They do not know the darkness and the heartaches; they only understand something clearly at last and joy and call it "luck," They do not see the long and arduous journey but only behold the pleasant goal and call it "good fortune." They do not understand the process but only perceive the result and call it "chance."*

Having a vision provides the propellant or the belief to see it come true. However, there's always going to be the naysayer(s) who will tell you that you don't have what it takes to make it a reality. Sometimes, if it is a close friend or relative, they will certainly remind you of those skeletons in your closet. You may excitedly launch your ship but understand that those winds and storms are going to come billowing against you. Trusting their possible caring attitude, you can make that mistake of lending a deaf ear to your unused capacity crying out within you saying, "You can do it!" If success was a piece of cake everyone would be successful, then there wouldn't be a reason to go through the cocoon and change. Unsuccessful people remain uncoordinated with success, mainly because they resist change. Ask any winner and they'll tell you that: The major difference between successful people and unsuccessful people is successful people master the art of bouncing back from failure. They keep on keeping on.

Do you know someone who started something but failed to finish it? I know so many would-be authors who begin drafting a book, yet they never finish. It under no circumstances makes its way out of their hard drive. They live a life of "if only I can, or I wish I did." Don't fall into that trap; it's always fully baited with excuses waiting for failures bent on quitting. Launch your dream and pursue it with reckless abandon. Harriet Beecher Stowe declared: "When you get into a tight place and everything goes against you, 'til it seems as though you could not hold on to a minute longer. Never give up then, for that is just the place and time that the tide will turn."

Back in my pre-writing days, I could have said "Let that major movie studio keep their film, do whatever they want to do with it. In Hollywood, it's a rat-race mindset anyway. I wasn't meant to be a writer in the first place. I came here only to act so I'll sit and wait for the auditions. No one wants to read about what I have to say. I'm a high school dropout and on and on… Instead, it was perfectly timed, a blessing in disguise – I heeded that call to write. In the book, The Tipping Point Malcolm Gladwell states: The world as we want it to be-do not accord with our intuition…Those who are successful at creating social epidemics do not just do what they think is right. They deliberately evaluate their intuitions.

If you were to interview the most successful people in the world, they would tell you that one of the keys to their overwhelming success is that they trusted their hunch. Yes, it's like fishing; they felt the nibble and tugged on the line. I believe that when God gives you a vision, he also gives you the ability, and in his timing, you'll certainly reach your destination if you persevere.

13

THE POWER OF BELIEF

One of the greatest acts of Belief was displayed by the Man who walked on water. When Jesus walked on this earth it was said he performed numerous miracles. He became the master of taking people from not having to have. He cleansed the person with leprosy, gave sight to the blind, fed the multitudes, restored a severed ear, calmed the stormy sea, walked on water, turned water into wine, and many more. Spectators and recipients saw this amazing power called belief at work firsthand.

The power of belief has also moved many individuals from the status of a nobody to a person of not only amazing success but true significance. It has also cured many individuals of fatal diseases, including cancer, as in the case of my pastor's wife. Belief is like a bridge that takes one from not having to have.
Though this imaginary bridge exists, still, many still lack the inspiration necessary to see beyond their present circumstances. Seeing beyond the horizon seems to be a foe instead of a friend urging them on. Additionally, their actions of yesterday tend to not only bring them to where they are now but also like taking a permanent pit stop. Thus, these actions keep them stuck, because like driving a car, they look in the rearview mirror versus the windscreen. Those same "wanna-be's" will tell you that they would do something to enhance their life *"but."* Thus, their too many "buts" only aid in keeping them where they are versus where they can be.
Believing in yourself has much to do with the value you place on your potential. If you see yourself as "a nobody" that's what you will

believe about yourself. Just like the saying goes, "garbage in garbage out" you will receive little instead of much.

I call these believers in you "ladder holders. "They wait, holding up the ladder, cheering you on to amazing success. They are looking for people who are willing to make that first step and the second and the third. In you, they recognize not only your amazing potential but your powerful belief. This attraction keeps them standing in the gap, holding onto the ladder until they arrive at the last rung.

A person of value also believes that he or she is among the best, therefore they act and perform at their best. They believe that they can remove mountains therefore they do so. Watch someone who is striving to become all they can be, and you will notice that instead of becoming less, they grow as a person because they are constantly working on themselves. They don't look for things to become easier, instead, they acquire the skills necessary to solve problems as they arise. They know that they are either in the middle of a problem, coming out of a problem, or getting ready to be faced with the next problem. Place a challenge in their path and watch it dissipate. Since they believe that they are resourceful they dominate as an analytical person.

Belief is very powerful; it can drive your thoughts. Believing that something is possible always triggers the mind to find a possible solution.

This reminds me of the story of David in Goliath in the Old Testament. David was matched up against this Philistine giant, who dared David to approach him. His peers probably saw a mountain in his way. David only saw Goliath as too big to miss. Because of this giant-sized faith in God, he slew the giant with a few stones and a slingshot.

What giants are standing in your way right now? Who or what is in your corner telling you that they can't be slain? Do **you** believe they can be slain? Or do you never see an end in sight? Belief, genuine belief, inspires one to do the impossible. Belief causes an individual to break bonds of restraint in his or her mind, to accomplish tasks in record-breaking style. They become resilient, inspired, and unstoppable!

I LOVE SPORTS. Not only are sports exciting to watch. Sports always bring out the combativeness in athletes. Michael Jordan, one of the greatest players to ever play the game of basketball, displayed tremendous belief in himself. In 1990, while playing for the Chicago Bulls, his inspiration helped him score three times his jersey number by dropping in 69 points against the Cleveland Cavaliers.

To become successful at anything, you first must believe that you can. Wishing will never put you in the driver's seat. Most often your belief can be stretched out like the waiting process involved in the growth of a Chinese Bamboo Tree. Understanding the growth process of this unique tree will certainly dispel those doubts and fears that you hold about yourself - those imaginary walls deterring you from ever becoming who you were always meant to be. In my opinion, this is a classic example of doubt and faith put to the test:

You take a little seed and plant, water, and fertilize it for a whole year, and nothing happens.
The second year you water and fertilize it, and nothing happens.
The third year you water and fertilize it, and nothing yet.
The fourth year you water and fertilize it, and still nothing.
The fifth year you continue to water and fertilize the seed. Sometime during the fifth year, the Chinese bamboo tree sprouts and grows NINETY FEET IN SIX WEEKS.

This power, based on your deep-rooted feelings about yourself, will harness your resolve and take you to insurmountable heights in your life and career. If you trust it, it will take you from the impossible to amazing success. *All things are possible to him who believes.* Mark 9:23.

If you have genuine faith, described as *"the substance of things hoped for, and the evidence of things not seen"* **which embodies belief - in yourself and the process. You are like a bodybuilder developing a robust body. You are ripped!**

14

FUELING YOUR THOUGHTS

After drafting my first book, I purposed to not remain a one-book-wonder. Encouraged by some well-meaning friends I'm always in search of the next investment, invention, design, book, or screenplay to marshal, cognizant of the fact that ideas release energy and my best work has not been born. *The more the mind does, the more it can do*, says William James.

Don't let one success – no matter how great – satisfy you. The Law of Creation, you know is the Law of Growth. You can't stand still. You must go forward – or be passed by. Complacency – self-satisfaction – is the greatest enemy of achievement. States, Robert Collier in *The Secret of the Ages: The Master Code To Abundance And Achievement.*

As we open the channels between our mind and the Universal Mind, there is no limit to thoughts of abundance that will manifest.

I have an affinity with these thought stimulants:

-*As a man thinks, so is he. (Proverbs 23:7) - I can do all things through Christ which strengthens me. (Philippians 4:13)*

-*No weapon that is formed against thee shall prosper…(Isiah 54:17)*

-*Jesus said unto him, If thou canst believe, all things are possible to him that believeth. (Mark 9:23)*

-*But indeed, I have raised you up, that I may show My power in you, and that my name may be declared in all the earth. (Exodus 9:16)*

-*Then this Daniel distinguished himself above the governors and straps because an excellent spirit was within him, and the king gave thought to setting him over the whole realm. (Daniel 6:3)*

-*I am the vine; you are the branches. Whoever abides in me and I in him, he it is that bears much fruit, for apart from me you can do nothing. (John 15:5)*

-*Brethren, I do not count myself to have apprehended; but one thing I do, forgetting those things which are behind and reaching forward to those things which are ahead. (Philippians 3:13)*

-For whatsoever is born of God overcomes the world. And this is the victory that has overcome the world – our faith.
(1 John 5:4)

If you want a thing bad enough to go out and fight for it, to work day and night for it, to give up your time, and your sleep for it...if all that you dream and the scheme is about it, and life seems useless and worthless without it...if you gladly sweat for it and fret for it and plan for it and lose all your terror of opposition for it...if you simply go after that thing you want with all of your capacity, strength and sagacity, faith, hope and confidence, and stern pertinacity...if neither cold, poverty, famine, nor gout, sickness nor pain, of body and brain, can keep you away from the thing that you want...if dogged and grim you beseech it, with the help of God, you WILL get it!

- Author Berton Braley

15

MAGNETIC THOUGHTS

When you move tenaciously in the direction of your vision, your vision moves tenaciously toward you. The truism screams: *No one can stop the man with a plan because no one has a plan to stop him.*
If you plan on launching out with your idea, confidence is always a zealous sidekick. As you launch out, you will not only see doors of opportunity swing open,

ushering you to a seat at the table but dream stealers as well.

Be prepared to own the room. It is like having your chocolate ice cream and knowing no one has the right to it but you. I love the TV show *Shark Tank*. You win big or go home.

Also, understand that dream stealers will emerge, even those close or closest to you could potentially attempt to derail your train if you let them. They don't see what you see for yourself. Plus, if they saw what you envisioned it might not be a feat they can accomplish. A magnet has two poles: one which repels and the other which attracts. However, because you stepped out, you have already beaten the odds. Your thought was likely given to someone else, but they didn't put that thought to work to profit from it.

Be ready to accept your transformation:

You are a living magnet, drawing to yourself the people, the resources, and the ideas you need to fulfill what you expect. To the successful it is out of their faith, for others, it is out of their fears. If you don't like what you attract, don't change what is coming towards you, change the magnet that is bringing those things into your life.

States, Scot Thomas Andreson.

Additionally, stay the course. Like a caterpillar, you have left the cocoon.

Nothing in the world can take the place of persistence. Talent will not. Nothing is more common than unsuccessful men with talent. Genius will not. Unrewarded genius is almost a proverb. Education will not. The world is full of educated derelicts. Persistence, determination, and hard work make the difference. States, Calvin Coolidge.

Oprah Winfrey was born in Mississippi at a time when segregation in that state denied basic civil rights to African Americans. She came from a home with no electricity and drinking water, also a victim of a troubled youth. As a child she was required to read books and every two weeks, to draft a report about what she had read. Oprah would often say that she wanted to make her living by talking. She was a gifted, quick-witted speaker, with pizazz.

In 1972 she became the first Black woman to hold the anchor position at Nashville's WTVF-TV. In 1986 she launched the Oprah Winfrey Show. In 1994 she bought her studio "Harpo." In 1996 she began Oprah's Book Club to promote reading, for which she recommended a recently published book each month. She sat aside one show each month for a full discussion on the book. She has since created her classic book club, which features three authors per annum. It is said: that Oprah regularly gives 10% of her income to charities, mostly having to do with youth, education, and books.

Oprah Winfrey, who became a billionaire at age 49, has not only risen to become the most powerful and influential woman in the television world but also ruler of a large entertainment and communications empire - from a life of poverty and abuse to a life of greatness. Oprah Winfrey at one point in her broadcast career believed in herself so much that sources close to her knew that she was like a hit record to be released. It wasn't long before she became that hit record. She has broken down so many walls because she thought she could. When she talks - people listen.

There are things you and I will accomplish in our lifetime that will not only affect our relatives, friends, neighbors, and co-workers but also our enemies alike.

It has been discovered that 90% of an iceberg rests beneath the surface. It may surprise you that each of us has at least 90% of our potential lying untapped. As human beings, we are known to use only that other 10% of our potential.

Mark Burg was born in 1959, in Hartsdale, New York. I first met Mark in 1997, when he and his 3year-old son JR became tenants in the building managed by my wife and me at the time. His son bonded with my sons Jonathan and Jefferri. While our sons engaged in sporting activities, Mark and I discussed filmmaking. Sometimes when he found it necessary to catch up on script reading, our kids found the Guardian in me.

Mark invited me to numerous events. Sometimes we took in a Clippers basketball game, and other times parties as well as film or TV sets for Two and a Half Men John Q and others. Mark has experienced a growing movie franchise, generating over $100,000,000 in the last five yearly installments. That franchise is now prepping for its eleventh installment. Failures, looking at his success say he was lucky. I have known him for over ten years and consider him someone with a tremendous work ethic. Before his big break, not only have I seen him reading screenplay after screenplay and novel after novel looking for the right one. I've even handed him scripts noticing his enthusiastic script-reading appetite. An acquaintance of mine additionally told me that one day he saw him on an airplane with over six scripts in his briefcase.

When the idea for the horror film was presented to him by a struggling producer who was office-less and sometimes officiated from my friend's office couch. My friend sold his property, put some money down on another, and used a portion to finance the film. The film has grossed over $100M in its first and subsequent installments. He used his mindsight instead of his eyesight when he purchased that piece of property. His initial investment has now brought him an excess of over $500,000,000, within the last five years. Some said that he was lucky. I don't believe in luck. Real success occurs when preparedness and opportunity meet.

One day before his big BREAK, my sons and I visited him. He asked if I could watch his son play in the backyard while he caught up on his script reading, and I obliged. In addition, when the film moved into production, I booked a role as an actor in a movie starring actor Denzel Washington and saw him engrossed in a novel that he read during the lunch break. Today he is one of the top independent producers in Hollywood and relishes a phenomenal lifestyle, one to be greatly desired.

In my interaction with successful people from all cultures and levels of society, I have discovered that they are not only specialists in their field but that they had at one point in their lives said yes to their potential by profiting from thoughts.

Our world has been searching for you. It needs people who are willing to step off the sidelines and into the game. It needs individuals to make a significant difference.

When you launch towards a goal, no matter the distance, you move down a corridor of time. As you move, doors of opportunity will open that you would never have been able to see unless you had stepped out!

- Scot Anderson

16

CAST YOUR NETS FOR ABUNDANCE

While Jesus walked along the shore of **Lake Galilee**, he saw two brothers who were fishermen, Simon (called Peter) and his brother Andrew, catching fish in the lake with a net. Expanding his group of disciples: "Come with me, said Jesus in Matthew 4:18. Verse 20 "At once they left their nets and went with him."

One night his disciples were fishing from a boat. The fish didn't bite. Their catch was zero. In the minds of Peter, Andrew, and those other disciples who were fishermen, it was a given: Fishermen were supposed to catch fish. They did not and no doubt engaged in a pity party, casting blame.

Suddenly, and miraculously, Jesus appeared on board the ship as their pow-wow crescendo. Ignoring their rhetoric, he instructed, that they give another try by casting their net on the other side. Allegedly, their thought source had encountered multiple impasses, PRIOR.

To Simon Peter, the fisherman director, Jesus said: *"Launch out into the deep and let down your nets for a catch."*

But Simon answered and said unto him, "Master, we have toiled all night and caught nothing: nevertheless, at Your word, I will let down the net."

And when they had done this, they caught a great number of fish, and their nets were breaking. So, they signaled their partners in the other boat to come and help them. And they came and filled the boats, so they began to sink. (Luke 5:4-7) His disciples were convinced the lake was dried up not of water but of fish. Not so, proved Jesus, who owns the cattle on a thousand hills and all the fish in the oceans. The fault did not lie with the fish but with his disciples' trajectory. They saw lack. Jesus saw abundance. Suddenly, there were more fish in their nets than they could manage. They moved from a mindset of zero fish to boatloads, causing them to require assistance from other fishermen on the sea.

THE TAKEAWAY

Take a self-inventory. In you are seeds of greatness. It is up to you to cultivate and turn them into your harvest. Remember, you attract to yourself the support necessary to profit from those thoughts you drop every single waking moment of your life.

CAN'T

Can't is the worst word that's written or spoken;

Doing more harm here than slander and lies;

On it is many a strong spirit broken,

And with it many a good purpose dies.

It springs from the lips of the thoughtless each morning

And robs us of courage we need through the day:

It rings in our ears like a timely-sent warning

And laughs when we falter and fall by the way.

Can't is the father of feeble endeavor,

The parent of terror and half-hearted work;

It weakens the efforts of artisans clever,

And makes of the toiler an indolent shirk.

It poisons the soul of the man with a vision,

It stifles in infancy many a plan;

It greets honest toiling with open derision

And mocks at the hopes and the dreams of a man.

Can't is a word none should speak without blushing;

To utter it should be a symbol of shame;

Ambition and courage it daily is crushing;

It blights a man's purpose and shortens his aim.

Despise it with all of your hatred of error;

Refuse it the lodgment it seeks in your brain;

Arm against it as a creature of terror,

And all that you dream of you some day shall gain.

Can't is the word that is foe to ambition,

An enemy ambushed to shatter your will;

Its prey is forever the man with a mission

And bows but to courage and patience and skill.

Hate it, with hatred that's deep and undying,

For once it is welcomed 'twill break any man.

Whatever the goal you are seeking, keep trying

And answer this demon by saying: "I can."

Edgar A. Guest.

WHICH THOUGHTS HAVE YOU DECIDED TO TURN INTO A PROFIT TODAY?

DAY ONE

1. _____
   _____
   _____

2. _____
   _____
   _____

3. _____
   _____
   _____

4. _____
   _____
   _____

5. _____
   _____
   _____

WHICH THOUGHTS HAVE YOU DECIDED TO TURN INTO A PROFIT TODAY?

DAY TWO

1. _____
   _____
   _____

2. _____
   _____
   _____

3. _____
   _____
   _____

4. _____
   _____
   _____

5. _____
   _____
   _____

WHICH THOUGHTS HAVE YOU DECIDED TO TURN INTO A PROFIT TODAY?

DAY THREE

1. _____
   _____
   _____

2. _____
   _____
   _____

3. _____
   _____
   _____

4. _____
   _____
   _____

5. _____
   _____
   _____

WHICH THOUGHTS HAVE YOU DECIDED TO TURN INTO A PROFIT TODAY?

DAY FOUR

1. _____
   _____
   _____

2. _____
   _____
   _____

3. _____
   _____
   _____

4. _____
   _____
   _____

5. _____
   _____
   _____

WHICH THOUGHTS HAVE YOU DECIDED TO TURN INTO A PROFIT TODAY?

DAY FIVE

1. _____
   _____
   _____

2. _____
   _____
   _____

3. _____
   _____
   _____

4. _____
   _____
   _____

5. _____
   _____
   _____

WHICH THOUGHTS HAVE YOU DECIDED TO TURN INTO A PROFIT TODAY?

DAY SIX

1. _____
   _____
   _____

2. _____
   _____
   _____

3. _____
   _____
   _____

4. _____
   _____
   _____

5. _____
   _____
   _____

WHICH THOUGHTS HAVE YOU DECIDED TO TURN INTO A PROFIT TODAY?

DAY SEVEN

1. _____
   _____
   _____

2. _____
   _____
   _____

3. _____
   _____
   _____

4. _____
   _____
   _____

5. _____
   _____
   _____

WHICH THOUGHTS HAVE YOU DECIDED TO TURN INTO A PROFIT TODAY?

DAY EIGHT

1. _____
_____
_____

2. _____
_____
_____

3. _____
_____
_____

4. _____
_____
_____

5. _____
_____
_____

WHICH THOUGHTS HAVE YOU DECIDED TO TURN INTO A PROFIT TODAY?

DAY NINE

1. _____
   _____
   _____

2. _____
   _____
   _____

3. _____
   _____
   _____

4. _____
   _____
   _____

5. _____
   _____
   _____

WHICH THOUGHTS HAVE YOU DECIDED TO TURN INTO A PROFIT TODAY?

DAY TEN

1. _____
   _____
   _____

2. _____
   _____
   _____

3. _____
   _____
   _____

4. _____
   _____
   _____

5. _____
   _____
   _____

WHICH THOUGHTS HAVE YOU DECIDED TO TURN INTO A PROFIT TODAY?

DAY ELEVEN

1. _____
   _____
   _____

2. _____
   _____
   _____

3. _____
   _____
   _____

4. _____
   _____
   _____

5. _____
   _____
   _____

WHICH THOUGHTS HAVE YOU DECIDED TO TURN INTO A PROFIT TODAY?

DAY TWELVE

1. _____
   _____
   _____

2. _____
   _____
   _____

3. _____
   _____
   _____

4. _____
   _____
   _____

5. _____
   _____
   _____

WHICH THOUGHTS HAVE YOU DECIDED TO TURN INTO A PROFIT TODAY?

DAY THIRTEEN

1. _____
   _____
   _____

2. _____
   _____
   _____

3. _____
   _____
   _____

4. _____
   _____
   _____

5. _____
   _____
   _____

WHICH THOUGHTS HAVE YOU DECIDED TO TURN INTO A PROFIT TODAY?

DAY FOURTEEN

1. _____
   _____
   _____

2. _____
   _____
   _____

3. _____
   _____
   _____

4. _____
   _____
   _____

5. _____
   _____
   _____

WHICH THOUGHTS HAVE YOU DECIDED TO TURN INTO A PROFIT TODAY?

DAY FIFTEEN

1. _____
   _____
   _____

2. _____
   _____
   _____

3. _____
   _____
   _____

4. _____
   _____
   _____

5. _____
   _____
   _____

WHICH THOUGHTS HAVE YOU DECIDED TO TURN INTO A PROFIT TODAY?

DAY SIXTEEN

1. _____
   _____
   _____

2. _____
   _____
   _____

3. _____
   _____
   _____

4. _____
   _____
   _____

5. _____
   _____
   _____

WHICH THOUGHTS HAVE YOU DECIDED TO TURN INTO A PROFIT TODAY?

DAY EIGHTEEN

1. _____
   _____
   _____

2. _____
   _____
   _____

3. _____
   _____
   _____

4. _____
   _____
   _____

5. _____
   _____
   _____

WHICH THOUGHTS HAVE YOU DECIDED TO TURN INTO A PROFIT TODAY?

DAY NINETEEN

1. _____
   _____
   _____

2. _____
   _____
   _____

3. _____
   _____
   _____

4. _____
   _____
   _____

5. _____
   _____
   _____

WHICH THOUGHTS HAVE YOU DECIDED TO TURN INTO A PROFIT TODAY?

DAY TWENTY

1. _____
   _____
   _____

2. _____
   _____
   _____

3. _____
   _____
   _____

4. _____
   _____
   _____

5. _____
   _____
   _____

WHICH THOUGHTS HAVE YOU DECIDED TO TURN INTO A PROFIT TODAY?

DAY TWENTY-ONE

1. _____

2. _____

3. _____

4. _____

5. _____

WHICH THOUGHTS HAVE YOU DECIDED TO TURN INTO A PROFIT TODAY?

DAY TWENTY-TWO

1. _____
   _____
   _____

2. _____
   _____
   _____

3. _____
   _____
   _____

4. _____
   _____
   _____

5. _____
   _____
   _____

WHICH THOUGHTS HAVE YOU DECIDED TO TURN INTO A PROFIT TODAY?

DAY TWENTY-THREE

1. _____
   _____
   _____

2. _____
   _____
   _____

3. _____
   _____
   _____

4. _____
   _____
   _____

5. _____
   _____
   _____

WHICH THOUGHTS HAVE YOU DECIDED TO TURN INTO A PROFIT TODAY?

DAY ONE

1. _____
   _____
   _____

2. _____
   _____
   _____

3. _____
   _____
   _____

4. _____
   _____
   _____

5. _____
   _____
   _____

WHICH THOUGHTS HAVE YOU DECIDED TO TURN INTO A PROFIT TODAY?

DAY TWENTY-FOUR

1. _____
   _____
   _____

2. _____
   _____
   _____

3. _____
   _____
   _____

4. _____
   _____
   _____

5. _____
   _____
   _____

WHICH THOUGHTS HAVE YOU DECIDED TO TURN INTO A PROFIT TODAY?

DAY TWENTY-FIVE

1. _____

2. _____

3. _____

4. _____

5. _____

WHICH THOUGHTS HAVE YOU DECIDED TO TURN INTO A PROFIT TODAY?

DAY TWENTY-SIX

1. _____
   _____
   _____

2. _____
   _____
   _____

3. _____
   _____
   _____

4. _____
   _____
   _____

5. _____
   _____
   _____

WHICH THOUGHTS HAVE YOU DECIDED TO TURN INTO A PROFIT TODAY?

DAY TWENTY-SEVEN

1. _____
   _____
   _____

2. _____
   _____
   _____

3. _____
   _____
   _____

4. _____
   _____
   _____

5. _____
   _____
   _____

WHICH THOUGHTS HAVE YOU DECIDED TO TURN INTO A PROFIT TODAY?

DAY TWENTY-EIGHT

1. _____
   _____
   _____

2. _____
   _____
   _____

3. _____
   _____
   _____

4. _____
   _____
   _____

5. _____
   _____
   _____

WHICH THOUGHTS HAVE YOU DECIDED TO TURN INTO A PROFIT TODAY?

DAY TWENTY-NINE

1. _____

2. _____

3. _____

4. _____

5. _____

WHICH THOUGHTS HAVE YOU DECIDED TO TURN INTO A PROFIT TODAY?

DAY THIRTY

1. _____
   _____
   _____

2. _____
   _____
   _____

3. _____
   _____
   _____

4. _____
   _____
   _____

5. _____
   _____
   _____

About The AUTHOR

John Alan Andrews hails from the islands of SVG in the Caribbean. He began his acting career in New York. In 1996 he took his craft to Hollywood. He appeared in multiple TV Ads campaigns, and films including John Q, starring Denzel Washington. Andrews later found his niche - writing coupled with filmmaking, and not only starred in but produced and directed some of his work which won multiple awards in Hollywood.

With over 76 books in his multi-genre catalog, including *Rude Buay* poised for a Jamaican production, Andrews is currently drafting *The PIPS Series,* which is a police procedural TV series slated for the Mediterranean enclaves. He has also Co-Authored with his sons *Jonathan Andrews* and *Jefferri Andrews*. His latest books *Atomic Steps* and *Make Every Thought Pay You A Profit* are favs among business leaders, and his twisted *NYC Connivers* legal thriller series appeals to both women and men ages 16 -85. *The Pips Series (Body in A Suitcase)*. Also, *Samuel A. Andrews – Legacy* (A Biography).

More of his work can be found at **ALIPNET.COM** or **ALIPNET TV**, his recently launched OTT Streaming Platform.

John Alan Andrews states:

"Some people create, while others compete. Creating is where the rubber meets the road. A dream worth having is one worth fighting for because freedom is not free; it carries a massive price tag."

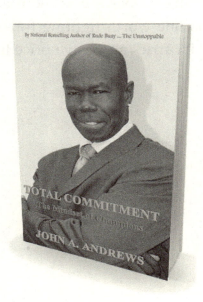

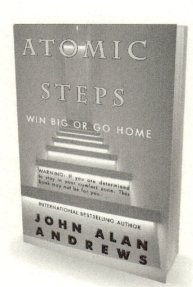

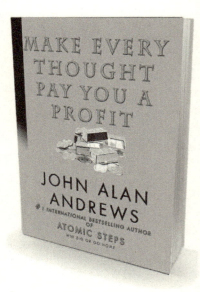

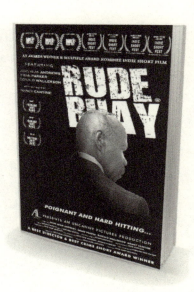
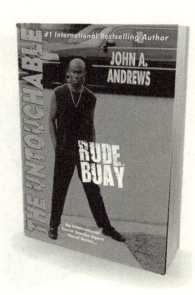
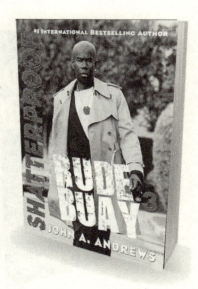

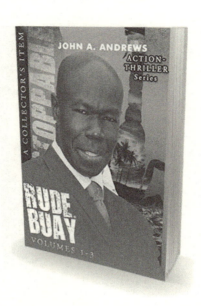
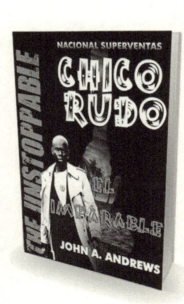
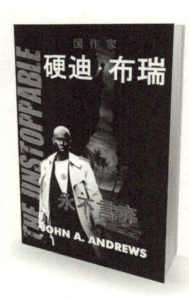

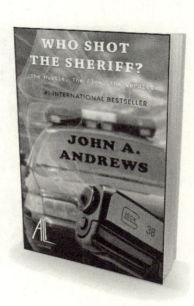
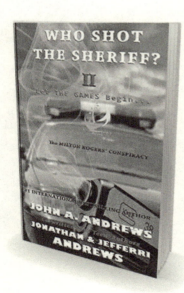
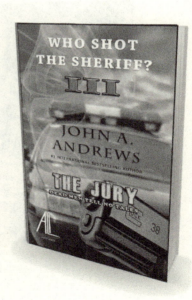

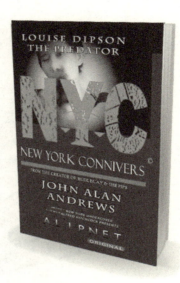
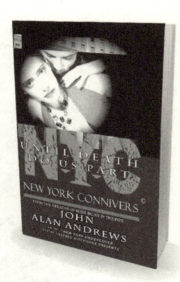
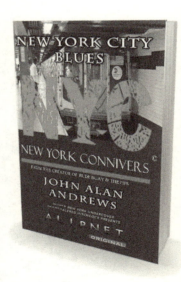

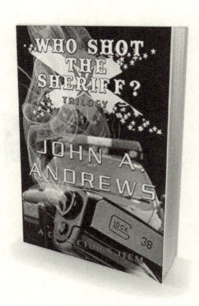
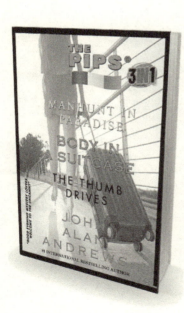
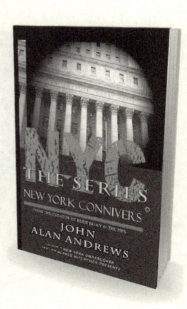

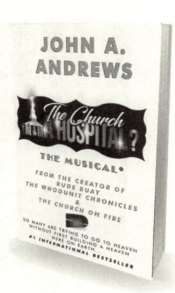
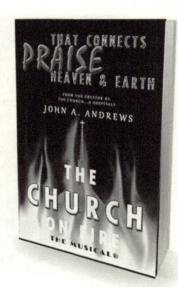
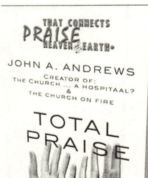

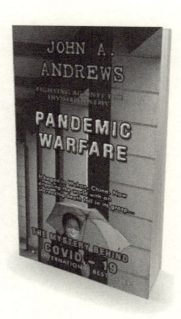

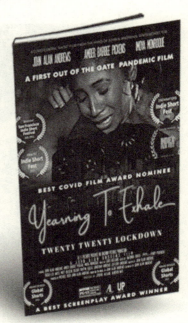

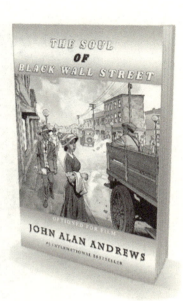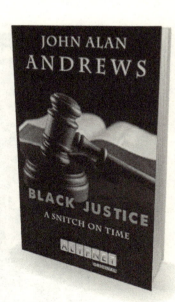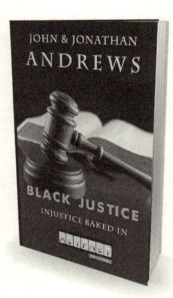

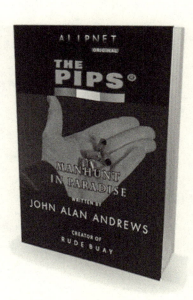
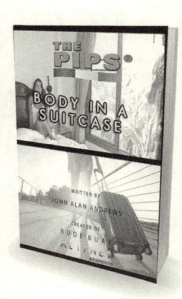
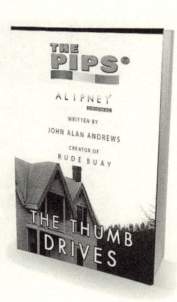

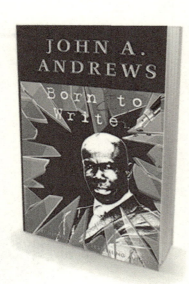
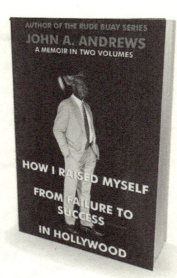

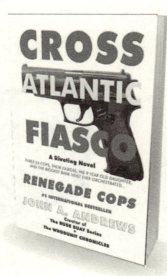
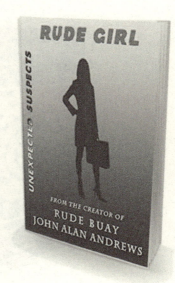

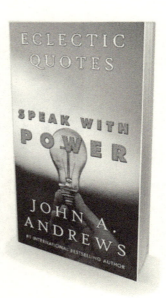

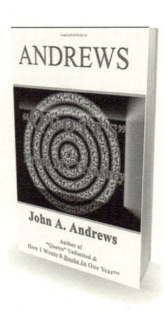

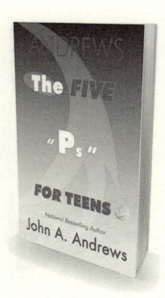

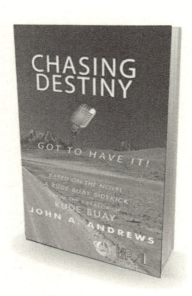
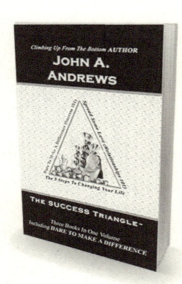

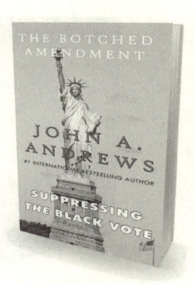
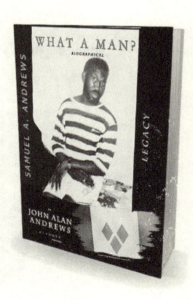
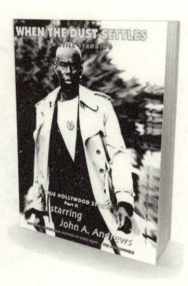

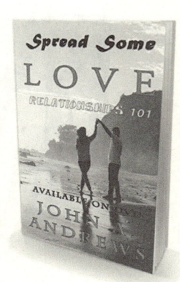
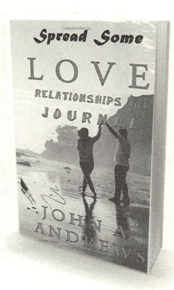

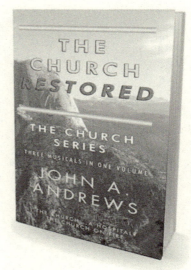

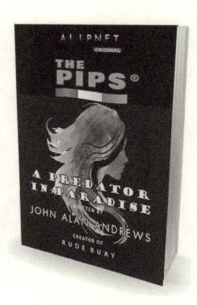
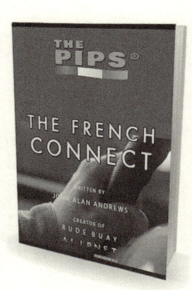
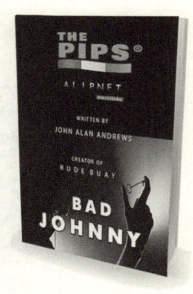

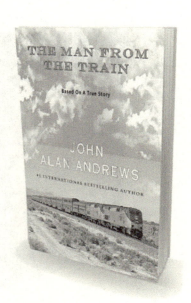

ALIPNET®
ORIGINAL

Made in the USA
Middletown, DE
05 January 2025

68133405R00081